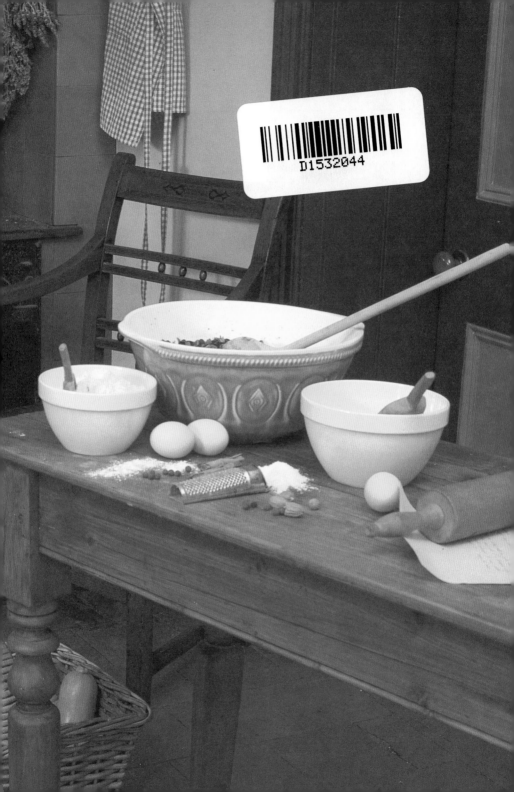

Marcia/Carol
1/20/95

The Country Kitchen

SAUCES

Jean Hatfield

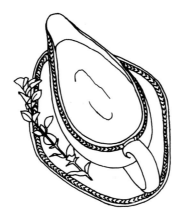

The Country Kitchen

SAUCES

Jean Hatfield

HARLAXTON
PUBLISHING

Front and back of jacket: A tasty display of sauces served at an outdoor lunch party. Brown sauce (p. 9), pesto (p. 44), French dressing (p. 40) and ice-cream cake with caramel sauce (p. 35).

Front and back endpapers: An old-fashioned country kitchen with the preparation for a spicy fruit cake in the foreground. The wood burning stove is wonderful for long, slow cooking.

Page 2: Melon balls with a most delicious lemon sauce (p. 47). Any type of melon can be used and a mixture makes for a very colorful dish.

 COOK'S NOTES: Standard spoon measurements are used in all recipes. All spoon measurements are level. All ovens should be preheated to the specified temperature.

Fresh herbs are used unless otherwise stated. If they are unavailable, use half the quantity of dried herbs. Use freshly ground black pepper whenever pepper is used; add salt and pepper to taste. Use all-purpose flour unless otherwise stated.

Published by Harlaxton Publishing Ltd
2 Avenue Road, Grantham, Lincolnshire, NG31 6TA, United Kingdom.
A Member of the Weldon International Group of Companies.

First published in 1992.
Reprinted in 1993.

© Copyright Harlaxton Publishing Ltd
© Copyright design Harlaxton Publishing Ltd

Publishing Manager: Robin Burgess
Project Coordinator: Barbara Beckett
Designer: Barbara Beckett
Illustrator: Amanda McPaul
Photographer: Ray Jarratt
Editor in United Kingdom: Alison Leach
Typeset in United Kingdom: Seller's, Grantham
Produced in Singapore by Imago

British Library Cataloguing-in-Publication data.
A catalogue record for this book is available from the British Library.
Title: Country Kitchen Series: Sauces
ISBN:1 85837 006 X

CONTENTS

Introduction
7
The Stocks
8
The Classic Sauces
11
Everyday Sauces
19
Tomato Sauces
28
Sweet Sauces
32
Sauces Made in a Blender or Food Processor
39
Index
48

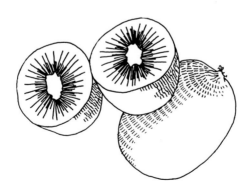

INTRODUCTION

GOOD SAUCES are an indispensable part of good cooking. The more one knows about their preparation, the greater the variety in ones cooking. You can use a sauce either to harmonize with and bring out flavor of a certain food or to provide a pleasant contrast to it. In either case, you can be guided by your taste, the ingredients you have on hand and the time you have available.

A good sauce produced with a minimum of effort is the wish of every good cook, so I have included recipes to make in a blender or food processor. With a blender not only can you make the popular white sauce and all its variations, but even difficult sauces such as mayonnaise can be made in seconds and are practically fool-proof.

If you are making sauce in the conventional way and it becomes lumpy, or if you are reheating a frozen sauce, a second or two in the blender will smooth it out. Take care not to blend a cooked sauce too long or it will become too thin.

Sauces do not need to be complicated or expensive–some of the tastiest sauces are the simplest and can be made with everyday ingredients. There is an art to sauce making and these recipes will show you how to master it.

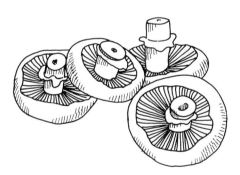

Barbecue sauce is quick and easy to make. It is always in demand to serve over broiled meat and poultry and will keep in the refrigerator for weeks. It tastes so much better than the bought variety and is better for you.

 COOK'S NOTES: Deglazing is one of the simplest and most rewarding ways to make a tasty sauce. Pour off any fat in the skillet or baking dish in which the fish or meat has been cooked and stir in a small quantity of liquid, such as stock, wine, cream or, at a pinch, water. Stir briskly to remove any sediment in the pan and cook over high heat to get the right consistency. For an extra sheen, swirl in a knob of cold butter and, when it has melted spoon the sauce over the food.

THE STOCKS

A WELL–FLAVORED and shiny sauce is often the result of a good stock. The stock is made with various bones, a few vegetables to flavor and the smallest amount of seasoning. The bones from a rare roast of beef will make a good brown stock. The bones from young animals contain the most gelatin, so try to include a few veal bones for a rich texture.

Brown Stock

2 1/2 pounds veal and beef bones
       A few black peppercorns
1   onion, roughly chopped
1   celery stalk
1/2   carrot
       Bouquet garni (comprising bay leaf,
       parsley stalks, sprig of thyme)
1/2   teaspoon salt

Wipe the bones and place in a baking dish. Bake in a moderate oven 325°F until well browned, about 20 minutes. Pour off the fat and put the bones in a large pan.

Add the remaining ingredients and pour in enough water to come three quarters of the way up the bones. Bring slowly to a boil and skim the surface. Reduce the heat and simmer gently for about 3 hours.

Strain the stock into a bowl and allow to cool before refrigerating. When the fat has set on the top; remove and discard. Keep the stock well covered and use when required.

Light Stock

This is the easiest stock to make and an excellent base for light sauces and gravies.

Make as for the brown stock, using veal or chicken bones or the carcass of a cooked chicken. For this, it is not necessary to brown the bones first. If making chicken stock, the giblets, excluding the liver, are also added.

Fish Stock

When you are buying fish ask the salesperson for some extra bones and fish heads. He or she will usually be happy to give them to you for nothing or for a few cents.

1 1/2 pounds or more fish bones
       and trimmings
1   tomato, chopped
       Parsley sprigs
1   bay leaf
1/2   large onion, sliced
1   garlic clove, crushed
2   teaspoons salt
6   black peppercorns
2 1/4 quarts water

Wash fish bones and trimmings well. Place in a large saucepan with all the other ingredients. Cover and bring to a boil. Reduce heat and simmer for 30 minutes. Strain and cool.

Fish stock can be stored in the freezer for several weeks and is excellent for making soup or sauces.

Brown Sauce

The basic ingredients for brown stock. The veal and beef bones have just come out of the oven and are about to be put into the stock pot along with the vegetables, herbs, salt, pepper and water.

Forming the basis for so many well-known sauces, it is made with a roux of oil and flour cooked to a good russet brown. Brown jellied stock is the best for this sauce.

2   tablespoons oil
1/4   cup each onion, celery and carrot,
         finely diced
1 1/2 tablespoons flour
2 1/4 cups brown stock
1   tablespoon tomato paste
         Bouquet garni (comprising bay leaf,
         sprig of thyme, parsley stalks)
         A few black peppercorns
         Salt and pepper

Heat the oil in a heavy pan and cook the vegetables until softened. Blend in flour and cook gently until well browned, taking care not to burn the onion. Remove from the heat and add 1 3/4 cups of the stock.

Bring to a boil, stirring well, and add remaining ingredients. Half-cover with a lid and simmer gently for about 25 minutes. Add half the remaining stock, bring to a rapid boil. Remove from heat, and skim off the scum that comes to the surface.

Repeat this process with the remaining 1/2 cup stock. This helps to give the sauce a good, clear shine. Strain through a fine strainer, press-

ing the vegetables well and reheat to use as required.

A good addition to this sauce is meat glaze set underneath the drippings poured off from a roast of beef. It keeps well in the refrigerator and is useful to have on hand for flavoring sauces and stews. Use about 2 tablespoons for this quantity of brown sauce.

If you keep a good store of brown stock, then brown sauce will be quick and easy to make. It is a great standby sauce for steaks, chops and sausages. Mop up the leftover sauce with crusty homemade bread and serve with a salad.

VARIATION
SAUCE MADÈRE is brown sauce with Madeira, to serve with steaks, lamb noisettes or cutlets. Heap one quantity of brown sauce and, just before serving, stir in 1/4 cup dry Madeira.

THE CLASSIC SAUCES

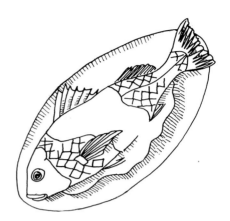

Béchamel (White) Sauce

Serve over vegetables and steamed fish.

1 1/4 cups milk
3   tablespoons butter
2   tablespoons flour
1/2   teaspoon salt
         Dash of pepper and ground nutmeg

Bring the milk to simmering point and set aside. Melt 2 tablespoons of the butter over low heat and stir in the flour. Cook for 1 minute. Do not allow to brown. Remove from heat and start adding the warmed milk gradually, stirring constantly. When you have added about half the milk return the pan to low heat and continue adding the milk and stirring all the time, taking care that your wooden spoon reaches right to the bottom and sides of the pan.

When all the milk is added, season with salt, pepper and nutmeg. Allow to simmer for 5-10 minutes, stirring occasionally, and just before serving beat in remaining butter.

You can vary the flavor of this sauce by using half stock and half milk, by adding a stock cube to the milk or by adding an onion, 2 cloves and a bay leaf to the milk, and allowing to stand for 20 minutes, then straining.

VARIATIONS
PARSLEY SAUCE: Make 1 1/4 cups béchamel sauce. Stir in 3-4 tablespoons chopped parsley and cook for 2-3 minutes. Serve very hot with boiled ham or corned beef, chicken or fish.

ONION SAUCE: Cook 2 medium sized chopped onions in 2 cups boiling salted water for 10-15 minutes. Make 1 1/4 cups béchamel sauce using half milk and half onion water. Add the well-drained onions and season with nutmeg. Reheat gently. Serve hot with roast lamb, boiled bacon and corned beef.

MORNAY SAUCE: Add 1/2 - 3/4 cup finely grated cheese to 1 1/4 cups béchamel sauce, and season with 1/2 teaspoon dry mustard and a dash of cayenne pepper. Stir or whisk gently until the cheese melts, but do not allow to boil or the sauce may become stringy.

Serve with macaroni, hard-cooked eggs, fish or vegetables.

OYSTER SAUCE: Make 1 1/4 cups béchamel sauce, using half fish stock if possible, or juice from oysters. Just before serving add 12 drained oysters and a squeeze of lemon. Reheat gently but do not allow to boil.

Served with baked or steamed fish.

Basic White Sauce

This is another version of this popular sauce.

1 1/4 cups milk
1/2 onion, stuck with a clove
2 tablespoons butter or margarine
2 tablespoons flour
   Salt and pepper

Pour the milk into a saucepan, add the onion and clove, and bring slowly to a boil. Draw the pan off the heat, cover with a lid and leave to infuse for 5-10 minutes. Disguard the onion and clove.

In a saucepan, melt the fat over a low heat and stir in the flour to make a smooth paste. This is called a roux. Cook the roux gently for a further minute or so, until it lightens in color and has a grainy texture.

Gradually stir in the warm, flavored milk a little at a time. Cold milk may be used if time is short, but warm infused milk makes blending easier and adds extra flavor. Each addition of milk should be thoroughly beaten in. Bring the sauce up to a boil and allow to simmer for 2-3 minutes to insure thorough cooking of the flour.

Season with salt and pepper and then add any flavoring required.

 COOK'S NOTES: Vanilla extract should ideally be added to mixtures when they have cooked and are cooling; heat will dissipate its delicate flavor. Real vanilla extract or extract has a far superior flavor to the imitation variety.
To make your own vanilla extract, chop a vanilla bean coarsely and place in a small bottle, cover with brandy, seal and store for about 3 months.

Hollandaise Sauce

Serve with broccoli, fish or chicken

1/2 cup butter, softened
2 tablespoons lemon juice
2 tablespoons wine vinegar
1 tablespoon water
2 extra teaspoons water
3 egg yolks
   Salt and pepper
   A pinch of superfine sugar, optional

Cut the butter into eight or nine pieces. Put the lemon juice, vinegar and water into a small saucepan. Boil briskly until the mixture is reduced to 2 tablespoons. Stir in 2 teaspoons cold water. Put into the top of a double boiler or into a glass or china pudding basin; set over a pan containing water that is just hot enough to tremble gently. Do *not* let the water boil.

Add the egg yolks. Keep the pan over a low heat and whisk until the egg yolks begin to thicken. Add one piece of butter. Whisk until it has melted. Add another piece of butter and continue whisking until it, too, has melted. Add piece after piece of butter until all the butter has been incorporated into the sauce and the sauce itself is thick enough to coat the back of a spoon.

If it has thickened too much, add 1-2 tablespoons cold water and make sure that the water in the pan under the sauce never boils. Season to taste with salt and pepper and, if liked, a pinch of superfine sugar. If preferred, all lemon juice may be used instead of vinegar.

 COOK'S NOTES: Ground spices, even if stored in an airtight container, require replacing every 12 months. Test the aroma of all ground spices before using.

Béarnaise Sauce

This sauce is made on the same principle as hollandaise but has a flavored vinegar base. Serve with steaks and seafood.

1 1/4   *cups white wine vinegar or dry vermouth*
1   *shallot, finely chopped*
  A few black peppercorns
1/2   *teaspoon dried tarragon*
1   *bay leaf*
  A sprig of thyme
2   *egg yolks*
1/2   *cup butter*
1   *teaspoon finely chopped parsley*
  Freshly ground white pepper

Place the vinegar or vermouth in a saucepan, preferably enamelled, with herbs and seasoning, boil rapidly until reduced to 1 tablespoon. Put the yolks in a bowl and strain on vinegar. Place over a pan of gently simmering water and whisk until thickened slightly.

Add butter gradually by slipping it through the fingers (slightly softening it) in small pieces. Whisk until butter is combined with the egg yolks and the sauce is thick and creamy. Stir in the parsley and season with pepper.

VARIATIONS

SAUCE CHORON: *Delicious with steaks or seafood, this is a béarnaise sauce lightly flavored with tomato paste, say about 1 tablespoon, and a squeeze of orange juice to taste.*

SAUCE PALOISE: *Served with roast or broiled lamb or broiled chicken, this sauce is made the same way as béarnaise with 1 tablespoon chopped mint leaves in place of the tarragon.*

Hollandaise sauce is a perfect sauce to serve with beef, seafood and lightly steamed vegetables.

Velouté Sauce (Velvet Sauce)

Delicious with steamed fish or chicken.

2   tablespoons butter
1 1/2   tablespoons flour
1 1/4   cups light stock (fish, chicken or veal)
        Salt and freshly ground white pepper
        Lemon juice to taste
1   egg yolk
1   tablespoon light cream

Melt the butter in a pan, remove from the heat and blend in the flour. Stir in the stock and slowly bring to a boil. Simmer gently for about 10 minutes and season with salt, pepper and lemon juice.

Combine the egg yolk with the cream and a little of the hot sauce. Pour back into the pan and allow to thicken slightly without boiling. Makes 4-6.

VARIATION
SAUCE POULETTE: *Serve this sauce with vegetables, especially carrots and broad beans. It also goes well with boiled veal.*
To 1 quantity of velouté sauce made from chicken or veal stock, add 2 teaspoons finely chopped parsley and an extra squeeze of lemon juice.

This delectable mushroom sauce made from velouté sauce marries well with roast lamb cutlets. It is a handy sauce for the busy cook because you can make it in advance and reheat when needed.

Mushroom Sauce

A nice accompaniment for steamed chicken.

2   ounces mushrooms
1   tablespoon butter
1/2 - 3/4 cup velouté sauce
1   tablespoon dry sherry, optional

Wipe mushrooms, slice if large and sauté quickly in butter. Add to velouté sauce with dry sherry and heat thoroughly. Serves 4-6.

Mayonnaise

There is no doubt about the popularity of this sauce and the mystery of how it is made has disappeared now that so many people own a blender or a food processor. I have given you the recipe for making this sauce in a blender on page 39 but, for those cooks who do not own this magic machine, here is the recipe. It is well worth the trouble to have a jar of homemade mayonnaise in the refrigerator.

2   absolutely fresh egg yolks
1/2   teaspoon salt
1-2   teaspoons Dijon mustard
1 1/4   cups olive oil or salad oil
1   tablespoon white vinegar or lemon juice

Put egg yolks, salt and mustard into a bowl. Beat vigorously with a wooden spoon until thickened. Add the oil drop by drop until 1/4 cup has been added. Stir in half the vinegar. As the mixture thickens pour in the remaining oil in a thin stream. It is important to keep stirring. When nearly all the oil has been used, taste the sauce and add as much of the remaining vinegar as you like. Unless you are going to use the sauce straight away, cover closely and store in the refrigerator. Here are some sauces that have mayonnaise as their basic ingredient.

Green Tartare Sauce

One of the best sauces for lobster salad or any other seafood. The parsley can be stored in a plastic container after squeezing, and used for decorating.

A small bunch of parsley
1   *cup mayonnaise*
2   *teaspoons chopped capers*
2   *slices eating apple, chopped, optional*
1   *tablespoon finely chopped celery*
1   *tablespoon chopped chives*

Rinse the parsley and chop very finely. This can be done in a blender. Dampen a corner of a clean dish cloth with a little water and place the parsley on the corner. Squeeze out the juice into the mayonnaise. Add the other ingredients and mix well. Place in a serving dish and hand round separately.

 COOK'S NOTES: This method of wringing parsley in a dish cloth can be used to color other sauces such as green butter. Cream butter and mix with 2 teaspoons of parsley juice, or enough to make a pretty color. Roll into a log, wrap in foil and store in the freezer. Cut into slices and serve with broiled fish or meat.

 COOK'S NOTES: If beating egg whites with an electric whisk, it is best if the speed is gradually increased until the half way stage and then returned to a slower speed so as not to dry out the egg whites. Egg whites should never be whisked to the point where they form clumps – when this happens, the eggs have been stretched to their maximum capacity and are likely to collapse when heated.

Cold Swedish Sauce

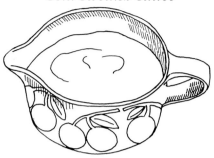

This is excellent with cold ham, salmon or any cold fish. It is a good idea to have a jar of apple purée (the kind that is made for babies) in the kitchen ready to open if you do not have time to make the apple sauce.

1   *cup mayonnaise*
2   *tablespoons apple sauce (p 19)*
2   *teaspoons horseradish relish*
1   *teaspoon superfine sugar*
2   *teaspoons Dijon mustard*
2   *tablespoons light cream*

Place all the ingredients in a bowl and mix well together. Taste, and season with salt if necessary. Store in the refrigerator until ready to serve. Serves 8-10.

Tartare Sauce

Serve with fried, broiled fish or poached salmon.

1/2   *cup mayonnaise*
1/2   *teaspoon Dijon mustard*
2   *teaspoons chopped parsley*
2   *teaspoons capers, chopped*
1   *hard-cooked egg, finely chopped*

Combine all the ingredients. If necessary you may thin the sauce with a little vinegar or lemon juice. Serves 4-6.

Ravigot Sauce

Another mayonnaise-based sauce which is excellent with lamb cutlets or broiled fish.

1	*cup mayonnaise*
1/2	*teaspoon anchovy essence*
1	*hard-cooked egg white*
1	*tablespoon each chopped parsley and capers*
1	*tablespoon chopped scallion*
1/4	*cup tarragon vinegar*

Mix mayonnaise with anchovy sauce and finely chopped egg white. Place capers, parsley and scallion in a small saucepan with vinegar, heat gently until boiling, allow to cool, and combine with mayonnaise. Chill before serving. Serves 6-8.

Tartare sauce is the perfect accompaniment for any type of fish, whether broiled, fried or baked.

Gribiche Sauce

This is a rich sauce resembling mayonnaise and is perfect for cold beef, tongue, chicken and broiled fish.

3	hard-cooked egg yolks
1	teaspoon Dijon mustard
1/2	teaspoon salt
	Freshly ground white pepper
1 1/2	cups olive oil
1/2	cup white wine vinegar
3	hard-cooked egg whites, finely chopped
1	tablespoon finely chopped mixture of parsley and tarragon

Gribiche sauce harmonizes well with cold meats, poultry and fish. I like the contrast with hot boiled meats as well.

Rub the egg yolks through a fine strainer. Mix with mustard, salt and pepper. Add olive oil gradually as if making a mayonnaise and then add the vinegar, stirring constantly. Finally add the egg whites, capers, gherkins and finely chopped herbs. Serves 6-8.

COOK'S NOTES: Sauce-boats add a lovely decorative element to the dining table as well as being immensely practical. Keep an eye out for them in thrift stores and at rummage sales.

EVERYDAY SAUCES

Lemon Cucumber Sauce

This is a good sauce for fish. You can leave the skin on the cucumber to give color.

4	tablespoons milk
	Juice of half a lemon
2	-inch piece of cucumber, diced
1	tablespoon flour
2	tablespoons butter
	Salt and pepper

Thoroughly combine all ingredients. Pour into a saucepan and bring to a boil, stirring constantly. Cook for 1 minute, adjust seasoning and serve. Serves 4.

Apple Sauce

Serve with roast pork, duck or pork chops. It also makes a refreshing dessert served with yogurt.

1	pound cooking apples
2	tablespoons water
2	teaspoons superfine sugar
1	tablespoon butter
	A pinch of ground cloves

Peel and core the apples. Slice into a saucepan and add the water. Cover and cook over a low to medium heat (if the heat is too high the apples will burn and stick) until the apples are soft and well broken down. Remove from the heat. Beat to a pulp, then add the sugar, butter and ground cloves. Beat well and serve hot. Serves 4-6.

Rarebit Sauce

The quickest sauce ever and makes a light meal with cauliflower.

1	cup Cheddar cheese, grated
1/2	cup milk
1	egg, beaten
1	teaspoon butter
1/2	teaspoon dry mustard
	A pinch of cayenne pepper

Melt cheese slowly in the milk. Add the egg, butter, mustard and pepper. Cook over boiling water, stirring occasionally, for about 7 minutes. Serve with cauliflower or steamed fish. Serves 4-6.

Mint Sauce

Serve with roast lamb, potatoes and green peas for a traditional British Sunday lunch.

1/2	cup mint leaves
1	tablespoon superfine sugar
2	tablespoons boiling water
3	tablespoons vinegar
	A pinch of salt

Wash mint leaves and chop them finely with a little of the sugar. Place in a sauce-boat or bowl and add boiling water. This will set the color. Stir in the sugar, vinegar and salt then leave to stand for 1 hour if possible. The sauce should be bright green in color and quite thick. Serves 6.

Bread Sauce

This old-fashioned sauce is coming back into favor now we know how important carbohydrates are in our diet. Serve with roast chicken, turkey and rabbit.

1 1/4	cups milk
1	bay leaf
1	small onion, sliced
2	garlic cloves
	A blade of mace or a pinch of nutmeg
3/4	cups white bread crumbs
1	tablespoon butter
1/2	teaspoon salt
	A pinch of pepper

Heat the milk. Add the bay leaf, onion, garlic and mace. Heat slowly and when nearly boiling, remove from heat, cover, then leave for 30 minutes. Strain the milk, combine with crumbs, butter, salt and pepper. Whisk over low heat until creamy and hot. 1-2 tablespoons whipped cream may be added if liked. Serves 6.

 COOK'S NOTES: Dried apricots are better cooked without sugar, as the sugar tends to toughen them. A little sugar may be added later.

Curry Sauce

An excellent sauce to use with hard-cooked eggs, canned tuna or shelled shrimp.

1/4	cup butter or ghee
1	apple, sliced
1	onion, sliced
2	teaspoons flour
2	teaspoons curry powder
1/2	teaspoon salt
2 1/2	cups stock, water or milk
	Juice of half a lemon

Heat the butter, add the apple and onion then fry until light brown. Add flour, curry powder and salt and cook gently for 5 minutes. Add the stock and bring to a boil, stirring constantly. Simmer gently for 15 minutes. Strain and add lemon juice.

Cumberland Sauce

One of the best cold sauces for cold ham, hot or cold duck and smoked tongue. Cumberland sauce can be safely stored in a sterilized jar for some time. It also makes a delicious gift for a lucky friend or relative.

2	tablespoons redcurrant jelly
1	tablespoon lemon juice
2	teaspoons Dijon mustard
1	tablespoon thick-cut marmalade
1	tablespoon dry sherry or port, optional

Mix all ingredients together roughly. Serve chilled. Serves 8-10.

Bread sauce is a traditional British recipe to serve with poultry and game. This is a very tasty version with the addition of onion and garlic. Add a few drops of Tabasco as well, if liked, or chopped parsley.

Peanut Sauce

You can use smooth or crunchy peanut butter for this simple sauce to be served with beef, lamb, pork or chicken satays.

1/2   *brown onion*
1   *garlic clove*
1   *small red chili*
     or a pinch of chili powder
1   *teaspoon peanut oil*
1/2   *cup peanut butter*
1/2   *cup milk*
1/2   *teaspoon superfine sugar*
     Salt
     Juice of half a lemon
     Soya bean sauce

Chop the onion, garlic and chili, and fry lightly in oil. Combine, peanut butter and milk, and

A very popular Italian recipe, garlic sauce has quite a few variations. In the picture above I added chopped red chilies and then half a cup of chopped parsley at the last minute.

add to onion mixture with the sugar and salt. Boil until the mixture thickens, stirring constantly.

Before serving add the lemon juice and soya bean sauce to taste. Garnish with fried onions and garlic. Serves 4.

Garlic Sauce

2-3   *garlic cloves, finely chopped*
1/4   *cup olive oil*
     Salt and pepper

Cook garlic gently in oil. Season and serve at once over well-drained hot pasta. Serves 4.

Hot Vinaigrette

Fine restaurants use this simple sauce to dress warm salads, simple meats and fish.

4	tablespoons olive oil
	or oil of your choice
4	tablespoons white wine vinegar,
	or 1/2 wine and 1/2 balsamic
	or sherry vinegar
1	tablespoon finely chopped shallots
	Pepper
1	teaspoon Dijon mustard
1	tablespoon chopped parsley

Heat the oil, vinegar, shallots and a fresh grinding of pepper. Whisk in mustard, add parsley and serve. Spoon over a warm salad and toss lightly.

Broiled or pan-friend chicken breast may be sliced, and served when still hot with a little hot vinaigrette to moisten.

Brush over chicken breasts, fish steaks or cutlets before broiling, baking or pan-frying, and serve with a little warm vinaigrette.
Serves 4-6.

Overleaf: Cilantro lime sauce (p. 28) about to be puréed in the food processor, ready to pour over fresh oysters. This is a refreshing new way to eat oysters, accompanied by thin slices of wholewheat bread and butter.

 COOK'S NOTES: Blanching nuts simply means removing their skins. To blanch almonds, cover them with boiling water, leave for 5 minutes, drain, and slip the skins off with your fingers. To blanch hazelnuts, roast them on a baking sheet in a moderate oven 350°F for 10 minutes. Tip the nuts onto a clean dish cloth and rub them together. Most of the skins will come off, but rub with the dish cloth if necessary.

Satay Sauce

This is a variation of peanut sauce that will keep in the refrigerator for several weeks. It is an excellent dip or used spooned over steamed vegetables.

2	tablespoons vegetable oil
1/2	cup whole peanuts, shelled
1	small onion, chopped
1	garlic clove, peeled and chopped
1	teaspoon terasi (dried shrimp paste)
	A pinch of chili powder
	Salt
1	tablespoon peanut oil
1 1/2	cups water
1	tablespoon tamarind water
1	teaspoon soft brown sugar

Heat the vegetable oil in a small skillet, add the peanuts and fry for about 5 minutes until just brown, shake the skillet constantly. Remove from skillet and leave to cool, then work to a powder in a mortar, blender or food processor.

Put onion, garlic and terasi (shrimp paste) in a blender or food processor and work to a very smooth paste. Add the chili powder and salt to taste. Mix well.

Heat the peanut oil in a pan, add the spice paste and fry gently for a few seconds, stirring constantly. Add water and bring to a boil, then add ground peanuts, tamarind water and sugar. Stir, then taste, adding more salt if necessary. Continue boiling until the sauce is thick, stirring constantly. Serves 4.

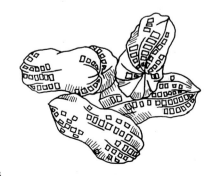

Cheese Sauce for Fish Fillets

An excellent sauce when time is short. Serve this tasty dish for a light lunch with a side salad.

1 1/2 pounds fillets of flathead or redfish
       Salt and pepper

FOR THE SAUCE
2   cups canned cream of celery
       or mushroom soup
1   cup Cheddar cheese, grated
1/4   cup sherry, optional
1/4   teaspoon paprika

Cut the fish fillets into serving pieces, removing any skin and bones. Season lightly with salt and pepper. Place in a greased, shallow ovenproof dish.

Combine the soup, cheese and sherry, and pour over the fish. Sprinkle with paprika and bake in a moderate oven 350°F for 25-30 minutes or until the top is golden-brown. Serves 4.

Ricotta Sauce with Pasta

3/4   pound pasta
6   ounces ricotta cheese, or fromage frais
1/2   cup parmesan cheese, grated
      Salt, pepper and ground nutmeg
1   tablespoon butter or margarine
      Finely chopped parsley or basil

Cook the pasta in salted boiling water until tender. Cream the ricotta cheese until smooth, add the grated parmesan and season with a little salt, pepper and a pinch of nutmeg. Place the drained pasta into a warmed serving dish and stir the cheese mixture into it. Add butter and place the dish in a warm oven for a few minutes. Garnish with finely chopped parsley or basil if wished. Serves 4.

Herb & Cream Sauce with Noodles

Pasta does not always have to be served with tomato sauce, and here is a very popular recipe from Northern Italy which is absolutely delicious. You can vary the herbs and use basil or oregano instead of rosemary but it is important to use fresh parsley and chives.

1   pound pasta noodles, fresh if possible
1/2   cup light cream
       Parsley
       Chives
       Rosemary
2   garlic cloves, crushed
1/4   cup butter
       Salt and pepper
       Freshly grated parmesan cheese

Cook the noodles in boiling salted water until just tender but so they still have a 'bite'. Drain thoroughly.

Heat the cream. Chop the herbs together coarsely and stir into the heated cream with half the butter and crushed garlic. Season to taste with salt and plenty of pepper. Add the cream to the noodles and toss lightly until mixed. Place in serving bowls, sprinkle liberally with grated parmesan cheese and remaining butter. Serves 4.

A very fast way to make a pasta sauce. Ricotta sauce tastes best with homemade tagliatelle. Tear up basil leaves to garnish just before serving. A perfect Saturday lunch in the garden.

Cilantro Lime Sauce

This is a change from the usual cocktail sauce. There is sufficient sauce for two dozen oysters and it is best freshly made.

1   *scallion, chopped*
1/2 *cup cilantro leaves*
1/2 *red chili, seeds removed*
4   *tablespoons freshly squeezed lime juice*

Place scallion, cilantro leaves, chilies and lime juice in a blender and purée for a few seconds. Store in a jar in the refrigerator and spoon over oysters just before serving.

Scotch Egg Sauce

Many of us know how good smoked cod is but have never served it with its own sauce.

1/3 *cup butter*
2   *tablespoons flour*
2   *cups milk, warmed*
3   *hard-cooked eggs*
      Salt and pepper
      A pinch of nutmeg

Melt half the butter in a saucepan, add flour and mix well over low heat. Do not allow to brown. Add the warmed milk, whisking constantly until smooth and creamy. Allow to simmer for a few minutes. Cut the eggs in half and sieve the yolks. Cut the whites into thin strips. Season with salt, pepper and nutmeg and thin the sauce if necessary with some of the milk or water in which the fish was cooked. Add the yolks and remaining butter cut into dice. Adding cold butter gives a shine to the sauce. Be sure the sauce is hot; then add the egg whites. Place the fish on hot plates and spoon the sauce on top. Serves 6.

TOMATO SAUCES

Cumin Tomato Sauce

A quickly made sauce to serve with broiled, fried or barbecued mullet or sea bream.

3   *ripe tomatoes*
2   *teaspoons cumin seeds*
2   *garlic cloves, crushed*
1/4 *cup white wine vinegar*
      A pinch of cayenne
1   *tablespoon chopped parsley*
      Salt

Drop tomatoes into boiling water and remove with a slotted spoon. Peel, core and cut in half. Gently squeeze the tomatoes to remove seeds, then dice finely. Place a heavy skillet over heat, drop in the cumin seeds and shake the pan until the seeds are toasted. Lower the heat and add the crushed garlic, tomatoes, vinegar and cayenne. Stir well and cook for 10-15 minutes until a good consistency. Add the parsley and salt to taste. Serves 6.

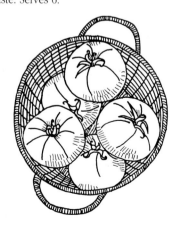

Tomato Chartreuse with Horseradish Cream

You can use fresh or bottled horseradish for this piquant sauce or, if neither is obtainable, dried horseradish powder is excellent–remember, however, to use half the quantity.

2 1/2 cups tomato juice
1 teaspoon tomato paste
1 garlic clove, finely chopped
1 bay leaf
1 sprig of thyme
6 black peppercorns
1 teaspoon superfine sugar
Salt
2 tablespoons water
1 tablespoon lemon juice
1 tablespoon gelatin

FOR THE HORSERADISH CREAM
2 tablespoons grated horseradish
A pinch of dry mustard
1 teaspoon superfine sugar
A pinch of salt
1 tablespoon wine vinegar
2/3 cup sour cream

Put the tomato juice and tomato paste into a saucepan with the chopped garlic, herbs and seasoning. Bring to a boil, take off the heat and leave to stand for 5 minutes.

Put the water and lemon juice into a cup and sprinkle in the gelatin. Allow to stand for a minute. Dissolve over hot water; then, add to the warm tomato mixture and mix well. When cold, strain into a wetted 2 1/2-cup ring mold and leave to set in a cool place.

For the horseradish cream, combine the horseradish, mustard, sugar, salt, vinegar and cream. To serve, dip the mold in a bowl of warm water for 5 seconds and turn out onto a dish. Place the horseradish cream in the center and serve with hot crisp rolls or melba toast. Serves 6.

Sicilian Tomato Sauce

A very popular sauce to serve with pasta. It is also always in demand at a barbecue as it goes well with barbecued meats, chicken and sausages. Add more chili if liked.

1 small eggplant
2 1/2 pounds ripe tomatoes
1/4 cup olive oil
2 garlic cloves, crushed
1 red chili, chopped
1 tablespoon chopped basil leaves
4 anchovy fillets
Salt and pepper
Basil leaves

Peel the eggplant and cut into dice. Place in a bowl, sprinkle with salt and leave for 30 minutes. Drain well, set aside. Place the tomatoes in a bowl; cover with hot water and leave for 1 minute. Remove from the water, peel, roughly chop and purée in a blender. Heat the oil and sauté the garlic until golden.

Add the eggplant, simmer for 5 minutes, stirring occasionally. Add tomatoes, red chili and basil and simmer; uncovered, for 40 minutes or until the sauce is thick. Add anchovies and simmer for a further 5 minutes. Season with salt and pepper. Garnish with fresh basil leaves. Serves 4.

 COOK'S NOTES: Just one or two drops of Tabasco sauce, made from very hot red peppers, can give an almost magical lift to sauces, especially seafood sauces.

Tomato Sauce

The simplest and perhaps the best of all sauces when made from ripe tomatoes. Serve over pasta, green vegetables or broiled meats.

1	*pound ripe tomatoes*
1	*tablespoon butter*
	Salt and pepper
1	*teaspoon superfine sugar*
1	*teaspoon chopped basil or parsley*

Pour boiling water over the tomatoes and peel. Chop the flesh roughly. Heat the butter in a heavy skillet or, add the tomatoes and cook quickly for 3 minutes–no longer. Season with salt, pepper and sugar. Add the chopped basil or parsley.

Piquant Tomato Sauce

Serve with broiled chops, steaks and sausages.

1	*onion, finely chopped*
1	*tablespoon butter or margarine*
1/4	*teaspoon white pepper*
2	*teaspoons superfine sugar*
2	*teaspoons Worcestershire sauce*
1/2	*teaspoon dry mustard*
4	*tablespoons tomato sauce from previous recipe*
2	*tablespoons vinegar*

Fry the onion in the butter until soft but not brown. Add the pepper, sugar, Worcestershire sauce, mustard, tomato sauce and vinegar, stir well, and bring slowly to a boil. Simmer for 2 minutes. Serves 4-6.

Homemade tomato sauce ready to be eaten with rose-mary and veal chops. What could be nicer?

SWEET SAUCES

HERE is a collection of the best 'dessert improvers'–most of them easy to make, and all of them delicious.

Apricot Sauce (I)

This goes very well with steamed puddings or baked rice.

2	tablespoons apricot jam
1	tablespoon lemon juice
2	teaspoons grated lemon rind
2	tablespoons hot water

Combine all the ingredients and chill.

Apricot Sauce (II)

This dessert sauce also makes a fine accompaniment to lamb or pork.

1/2	pound dried apricots
1/2	cup superfine sugar
1	cinnamon stick, optional
2	teaspoons lemon juice or orange liqueur

Soak apricots for several hours in enough water to cover. Put them in a saucepan with cinnamon stick and bring to a boil. Lower the heat and simmer until the apricots are soft. Remove the cinnamon. Put the apricots into a blender and blend on medium speed until smooth. Add sugar, return to the saucepan and cook over low heat until the sugar has dissolved. Add lemon juice or orange liqueur. A little more water may be added if the sauce is too thick. Serve hot or cold. Makes 1 1/2 cups.

Cornstarch Sauce

This simple sauce is extremely popular with steamed puddings.

2	tablespoons cornstarch
1 1/2	cups milk
2	tablespoons superfine sugar
1/2	teaspoon vanilla extract

Blend the cornstarch with a little milk. Heat the remaining milk with sugar. Stir in the cornstarch and vanilla, and bring to a boil, stirring constantly. Cook for 3 minutes over very low heat.

Other flavors may be used in place of vanilla. Try peppermint or almond essence or 1 teaspoon grated orange or lemon rind. Serves 6.

VARIATIONS:
CUSTARD SAUCE: *Whisk 1 egg or 2 egg yolks into the above after cooking the cornstarch. Do not boil.*

CREAMY CHOCOLATE SAUCE: *Melt 2 squares chocolate in the milk before thickening or blend 1 tablespoon cocoa powder with milk and whisk in 2 teaspoons butter.*

Burnt Wine Sauce

A simple sauce that can be served hot or cold. Very good with sponge puddings, baked apples, baked rice or ice-cream.

2	tablespoons butter
3/4	cup superfine sugar
1/2	cup water, warmed
1/4	cup Port or sweet sherry

Apricot sauce II poured over sponge cake and vanilla ice-cream.

Place the butter and sugar in a heavy saucepan over gentle heat until golden-brown, stirring as little as possible. Add the water and the wine. Stir and bring to a boil. Cook for a minute or until the sauce is smooth.
Serves 4-6.

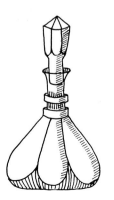

Jam Sauce

Another homely sauce to serve with steamed or baked puddings or pancakes.

2	tablespoons apricot, plum or raspberry jam
3/4	cup water
	Grated rind and juice of half a lemon
1	teaspoon cornstarch
1	tablespoon water

Place the jam, water, lemon rind and juice in a small saucepan and heat gently. Mix the cornstarch and remaining water, add to the jam and bring to a boil. Cook for 1 minute. Serve hot. Serves 4-6.

Peach Sauce

This sauce is delicious with ice-cream or lightly poached fruit. The sauce is best made just before serving.

4   ripe freestone peaches
2   teaspoons superfine sugar
1/4 cup sweet sherry

Lower the peaches into a saucepan of boiling water for 1 minute; then lift out of the pan into a bowl of cold water. While still warm, remove the skins, cut in half and discard the pits. Purée in a blender with the sugar. Add the sherry; cover and place in the refrigerator until ready to serve. Serves 4.

Fudge Sauce

A great sauce for ice-cream

1/2 cup soft brown sugar
2   tablespoons butter
2   tablespoons light corn syrup
4   tablespoons evaporated milk

Place all the ingredients in the top of a double boiler or in a bowl set over hot water, and stir well until melted, then spoon over ice-cream. Serves 4-6.

A dark caramel sauce poured over ice-cream and sponge cake. Guaranteed a dinner party success.

Melba Sauce (Berry Coulis)

Fortunately, raspberries and peaches arrive in the market at the same time so that all-time favorite, Peach Melba, can be enjoyed. The modern name for this berry sauce is coulis.

1/2 pound raspberries
2   tablespoons confectioners' sugar

Pick the berries over and place in a bowl over boiling water. Mash with a potato masher or wooden spoon. You can purée them in a blender, but I find this makes the sauce too frothy. Stir in the sugar and push the berries through a nylon strainer. Taste and add a little lemon juice or white wine, if liked. Keep the taste sharp as a contrast. Store in a plastic container until ready to serve over peaches and ice-cream.

You can vary the sauce by adding redcurrants or using strawberries. Serves 4.

Ice-Cream Cake with Caramel Sauce

This ever popular caramel sauce will keep in the refrigerator for a week and is good over steamed puddings as well as ice-cream.

2   tablespoons butter
1   cup firmly packed brown sugar
1/2 cup canned reduced cream
     Sponge cake
     Ice-cream

Melt the butter over low heat, add the sugar and stir well. Add the reduced cream and stir until it dissolves. Place a square of sponge cake in each serving glass and top with scoops of ice-cream. Spoon the sauce on top. Serves 6.

Grand Marnier Sauce

This must be the most delicious sauce to serve with strawberries or sliced fresh peaches.

5	*egg yolks*
1/2	*cup superfine sugar*
1/2	*cup Grand Marnier*
1	*cup heavy cream, lightly whipped*

Put the egg yolks and sugar into a bowl that will rest snugly on top of a slightly larger saucepan. Bring about 2-inches of water to simmering heat in the saucepan and place the bowl on top. With a rotary beater or hand-held electric mixer beat the egg yolks, making sure you scrape around the bottom of the bowl. A plastic spatula is useful for this. Keep beating for about 10 minutes until the yolks are thick and a pale lemon color. Do not allow the water in the saucepan to touch the bowl of egg yolks. Remove the bowl from the pan and stir in half the Grand Marnier. Cover the surface of the sauce with plastic wrap, allow to cool, then chill. Before serving, stir in the remaining Grand Marnier and fold in the cream. Serves 8-10.

 COOK'S NOTES: Cream for whipping must be chilled, the bowl and whisk should also be cold.
If an electric whisk is used, turn the setting to medium and whip until the cream begins to thicken, then lower the speed until soft peaks form. Cream thickens quite quickly.

Sauce Sabayon aux Fruits

A delicious sauce to serve with fruit at a special dinner party.

2	*egg yolks*
1	*tablespoon superfine sugar*
2/3	*cup sweet sherry*
	A strip of lemon peel

Put all the ingredients in a small bowl and stand it over a saucepan of simmering water. Whisk briskly until the sauce becomes thick and mousse-like. Do not allow the water to boil or the sherry will curdle the egg. Remove the lemon peel and serve immediately.

Pour over poached fruits such as pears, peaches or apricots. Serves 4-6.

Zabaglione

Zabaglione must not be cooked over direct heat. Be sure to choose a large enough bowl as the mixture will increase greatly in volume as you beat.

4	*egg yolks*
1/2	*cup superfine sugar*
	A squeeze of lemon juice
4	*tablespoons Marsala or sweet sherry*

Break the egg yolks into a bowl and mix lightly. Add sugar, lemon juice and Masala or sherry. Place the bowl over a saucepan of boiling water, then draw the pan off the heat. Whisk until the mixture is quite thick and fluffy.

Remove the bowl and pour the mixture into large goblets or glasses.

Traditionally, this sweet is served hot, as soon as it is made, with sponge fingers. Often poured over strawberries, peeled peaches or compote of fruit or served cold. Serves 6.

Sauce sabayon aux fruits makes a delectable dessert poured over pears in spiced red wine.

Custard Sauce

Steamed puddings are still a popular winter treat and I find this custard sauce is a great accompaniment.

1/2   cup superfine sugar
2   tablespoons custard powder
1   egg, beaten
3   cups milk

Combine the sugar, custard powder, egg and enough milk to make a smooth paste. Heat the remaining milk in a saucepan until almost boiling. Add the custard powder mixture and, stirring vigorously, bring to a boil. Pour into a serving jug. A tablespoon of brandy can be added if you wish. Serves 6.

The ever popular sweet sauce, custard, never fails to please. Here it is poured hot over a steamed fruit pudding.

Brandy or Rum butter

Serve with plum pudding at Christmas. This sauce can be made days in advance

1/3   cup butter
1   cup confectioners' sugar
2   teaspoons brandy or rum,
       or more to taste

Cream butter until soft. Sift sugar, add to butter and beat until white and light. Work brandy or rum into the mixture, then chill. Serves 6-8.

 COOK'S NOTES: The best method of adding cream to hot drinks such as Irish Coffee is to sweeten the coffee and pour the cream over the back of a spoon held with its tip on the surface of the coffee. This forms a layer of cream on top which helps to keep the drink beneath piping hot.

SAUCES MADE IN A BLENDER OR FOOD PROCESSOR

Hollandaise Sauce

Hollandaise sauce is the classic accompaniment to asparagus and fish and is served just warm. It is easy to make in a blender with a narrow goblet. If your blender goblet is wider at the bottom than the top, you may find the sauce doesn't thicken sufficiently. If so, pour the contents of the goblet into a bowl, place over gently simmering water and stir until thickened. Don't let the water boil. Be sure the melted butter is very hot but not browning.

3   egg yolks
1   tablespoon lemon juice
1   tablespoon water, wine or white vinegar
1/4   teaspoon salt
      Freshly ground white pepper
1/2   cup butter

Put egg yolk, lemon juice, water, salt and pepper into the blender. Cover and blend on high speed for a few seconds. Heat the butter until it begins to bubble. Add the melted butter very slowly to the egg yolk mixture while blending on high speed, until creamy. Adjust seasoning. Makes about 1 cup.

VARIATION
SAUCE MOUSSELINE: To the basic hollandaise sauce recipe add 2 tablespoons whipped cream just before serving with vegetables or seafood.

Blender Mayonnaise

2   eggs
1/2   teaspoon salt
      A pinch of white pepper
1   teaspoon Dijon mustard
1   teaspoon vinegar
1   cup oil, or other salad oil

Put all ingredients, except oil, into the blender, blend for a few seconds, then gradually add the oil through the feed tube, with the blender running at high speed. When all the oil is incorporated, add 2 more teaspoons of vinegar or lemon juice and switch off.
Makes about 1 cup.

 COOK'S NOTES: Fines herbes is the French term for a mixture of herbs for flavoring omelets, savory sauces and other dishes. The traditional mixture is parsley, chervil, tarragon, and sometimes chives, but other mixtures of fresh herbs may be used.

French Dressing

Although you can store French dressing, it is really at its best when freshly made.

2 teaspoons Dijon mustard (optional)
2 tablespoons wine vinegar
1 garlic, clove
   Salt and pepper
4 tablespoons oil

Put all the ingredients except the oil into the blender. Cover and blend at high speed for 30 seconds. Reduce speed to medium and gradually add the oil until well blended. Makes about 1/2 cup.

Mint Sauce

A traditional British sauce for roast lamb. A dash of it in gravy gives a lift.

   A handful of fresh mint leaves
1 tablespoon superfine sugar
2 tablespoons boiling water
3 tablespoons wine vinegar
   A pinch of salt

Put all ingredients into the blender and blend on low speed until the mint leaves are finely chopped. Leave to stand for at least 1 hour to allow the flavor to develop. Makes about 3/4 cup.

 COOK'S NOTES: Sauces made from fresh horseradish should be prepared a few hours before using so that its flavor has time to develop and blend into the added cream. Never put horseradish sauce into a silver dish-it will turn a very nasty color.
A glass or pottery dish is best.

Sour Cream Dressing

A delicious sauce for coleslaw or potato salad.

2/3 cup sour cream
1   tablespoon French dressing
1   small carrot, sliced
1/2 teaspoon celery seeds
1/4 teaspoon salt
1   teaspoon lemon juice
2   teaspoons chopped chives

Put all ingredients into the blender, cover and blend on low speed for 10 seconds. Scrape down, then blend on high speed for 10 seconds. Makes about 1 cup.

Low-Calorie Dressing

This is an excellent dressing for those on a low-calorie diet. It will keep in the refrigerator for a week and is used for coleslaw or potato salads.

3   tablespoons skim milk powder
2   tablespoons cold water
3-4 tablespoons lemon juice
2   teaspoons tomato ketchup
1/2 teaspoon chili or Worcestershire sauce
1/2 teaspoon prepared mustard
     A pinch of garlic salt
1   tablespoon finely chopped parsley
1   tablespoon finely chopped chives
     Artificial sweetener

Place milk powder and water in the blender and blend on medium speed until well mixed. Add all the other ingredients and blend at the same speed until thoroughly combined. Sweeten to taste. Makes about 1 cup.

French dressing ready to be poured over a mixed green salad. Dress the salad just before serving, otherwise the lettuce leaves will wilt.

Barbecue Sauce

This sauce will keep in the refrigerator for several weeks and can be used as a marinade.

1	*cup tomato juice*
4	*tablespoons tomato ketchup*
1	*tablespoon dry mustard*
1	*large onion, roughly chopped*
1	*garlic clove*
2	*tablespoons Worcestershire sauce*
2	*tablespoons vinegar*
1/2	*teaspoon salt*
2	*teaspoons superfine sugar*
	A strip of lemon peel
	Pepper

Put all the ingredients into the blender and blend on high speed until sauce is quite smooth. Pour into a saucepan, bring to a boil and simmer for 5 minutes. Cool and store in a large jar until ready to use.
Makes about 1 1/2 cups.

 COOK'S NOTES: Canned anchovies impart a delightful sharpness to many sauces and dressings but are very salty. Before using, soak the fish in milk for 30 minutes.
Anchovy butter is an excellent accompaniment to many fish and egg dishes. Beat butter with either anchovy fillets or sauce, season with lemon juice and pepper, form into rolls, and chill.

Sweet & Sour Sauce

Very good with fried fish, broiled shrimp or canned tuna fish.

2	*tablespoons superfine sugar*
6	*teaspoons cornstarch*
1	*tablespoon soy sauce*
3	*tablespoons vinegar*
1	*tablespoon tomato paste*
	A pinch of salt
1 1/4	*cups water*
3	*pineapple slices, chopped*
1	*small onion, finely chopped*

Put all the ingredients except the pineapple and onion into the blender and blend on high speed for 30 seconds. Put into a saucepan and cook gently until sauce thickens, stirring well. Add the pineapple and onion, cook for 3 minutes. Serves 6.

COOK'S NOTES: To peel a tomato, lower it into a pot of boiling water, count to six, remove it and place into cold water. Cut out the stalk end of the tomato with the point of a small knife. Make a nick in the skin and pull it off. To seed the tomato, cut in half crosswise and squeeze seeds out gently.

Sweet and sour sauce ready to be added to stir-fried pork, fish cubes or chicken pieces.

Pesto

A luscious, green, nutty sauce from Italy to eat with pasta, soup or as a sauce with meats and poultry.

4   *cups basil leaves, washed*
5   *garlic cloves*
2   *tablespoons pine nuts*
     Salt and pepper
     Olive oil
1/2 *cup grated parmesan cheese*

In a food processor, blend together the basil, garlic and pine nuts then season with salt and pepper. Gradually add olive oil until the sauce is smooth and thick. Pour into a bowl and mix the parmesan cheese in with a wooden spoon.

Apple Sauce

This classic sauce for roast pork is also very good with sausages.

1   *pound cooking apples*
3   *tablespoons water*
2   *teaspoons superfine sugar*
1   *tablespoon butter*

Peel and core the apples. Slice into a saucepan and add water. Cover and cook over low to medium heat until the apples are well broken down and soft. Remove from the heat. Place in a blender and blend on medium speed until smooth. Add the sugar and butter and stir until the butter has melted. Serve hot or cold.

Pesto has been called the food for lovers. It is truly one of the simplest and greatest delights of Italian cooking. It is best served with thin, homemade tagliatelle.

Ravigot Sauce

This tasty sauce can be made in the blender and is excellent with broiled fish. It is also good as a sandwich filling or a topping for crackers.

> *A big bunch of mixed fresh herbs*
> *(parsley, chives, chervil, thyme,*
> *lemon thyme, tarragon)*
> 2   *teaspoons capers, chopped*
> 2-3   *anchovy fillets, chopped*
> 1   *egg yolk*
>   *Salt and pepper*
>   *Oil*
>   *Vinegar*

In the blender, chop herbs together very finely. Add the capers and anchovies. Season with salt and pepper. Stir in the egg yolk. Gradually add 2-3 tablespoons oil, then a little vinegar.

COOK'S NOTES: *Fresh basil leaves will bruise easily and should be either torn with the fingers or cut with a sharp stainless steel knife. It is best to add this herb to a sauce or salad just before serving.*

Ricotta Herb Sauce

This sauce is easy to prepare and is delicious with any hot pasta, as a spread on toast, or for sandwiches.

> 1/3   *cup pine nuts, toasted*
> 1/4 -   1/3 *cup Spanish or good olive oil*
> 2   *tablespoons chopped cilantro*
> 1/2   *garlic clove, crushed*
> 1   *tablespoon marjoram*
> 1/2   *cup ricotta cheese*
>   *Pepper*

Place nuts, oil, cilantro, garlic and marjoram in a food processor and work until smooth. Add the ricotta and work for 10 seconds. It will keep in the refrigerator for several days.
Serves 6.

Curry Sauce

This sauce is good with pasta or rice.

> 2   *tablespoons butter*
> 1   *tablespoon oil*
> 1   *carrot, roughly chopped*
> 1   *garlic clove*
> 1   *small potato, roughly chopped*
> 2   *teaspoons curry powder*
> 1   *teaspoon tomato paste*
>   *Salt*
>   *A few drop of lemon juice*
> 1 1/4   *cups chicken stock*

Melt the butter in a saucepan, add the oil and sauté vegetables for about 5 minutes, stirring constantly. Increase the heat, add the curry powder and cook for a further 1-2 minutes. Put into the blender and blend on high. Add the lemon juice and some of the stock. Blend on high speed for a few seconds. Return to the saucepan with the remaining stock and simmer for 10 minutes. Makes about 1 1/2 cups.

Custard Sauce

Serve with steamed puddings, poached fruit and apple pie.

2	egg yolks
2	tablespoons superfine sugar
1/2	teaspoon vanilla extract
1	teaspoon cornstarch
1	cup milk

Put the egg yolks, sugar, vanilla extract and cornstarch into a blender and blend on low speed until mixed. Bring the milk almost to boiling and pour slowly back into the blender. blend on low speed for a few seconds. Return to the saucepan and cook gently until custard comes to a boil and thickens.
Makes about 1 cup.

Lemon or Orange Sauce

Serve with pancakes, steam puddings or ice-cream.

1	small orange or lemon
1 1/4	cups water
1/4	cup superfine sugar
2-3	tablespoons cornstarch

Pare the zest from the orange or lemon as thinly as possible. Place in the blender. Remove the peel and pith from the fruit then cut up. Put into the blender with the zest. Add remaining ingredients and blend on high speed until the zest is finely chopped. Pour into a saucepan and stir until the mixture comes to a boil. Boil for 3 minutes. Serve hot or cold.

Lemon Sauce with Melon Balls

Choose a ripe melon for this first course.

1	honeydew or cantaloupe melon
2	lemons
	A little water
1-2	tablespoons superfine sugar
	Sprigs of mint
	Lemon twists

Halve the melon, remove the seeds.
Take a melon baller, scoop out the flesh and chill the balls. The rather untidy pieces at the bottom of the fruit can be used for the sauce. Grate about 2 teaspoons of rind from the lemons. Squeeze the juice, measure, and add enough water to give 2/3 cup.
Simmer the rind with the liquid and sugar for about 5 minutes. Pour over the odd pieces of melon, then blend in the blender.
Taste and add more sugar if wished, but it should not be necessary as the sauce ought to be both thick and fairly sharp. Spoon into the bottom of individual glasses and top with the melon balls. Garnish with mint and lemon.
Serves 4-6.

Chocolate Sauce

A 5-minute sauce for steamed or baked puddings.

1 1/4	cups milk
6	teaspoons cornstarch
2	tablespoons superfine sugar
2 1/2	tablespoons cocoa powder

Put all the ingredients in the blender and blend at high speed for 10 seconds. Put into saucepan and bring to a boil, stirring all the time. Cook for 3 minutes or until the sauce thickens.

INDEX

Page numbers in **bold** type indicate illustrations.

Anchovy 43
anchovy butter 43
apple sauce 19
  blender or processor recipe 44
apricot: dried 20
  sauces 32, **33**
Barbecue sauce 6, 43
basic white sauce 12
basil 46
béarnaise sauce 13
beating egg whites 17
béchamel (white) sauce 11
berry coulis 35
blanching nuts 23
brandy butter 38
bread sauce 20, **21**
brown sauce 9, **10**
brown stock 8, **9**
burnt wine sauce 32
Caramel sauce 35
cheese sauce for fish fillets 26
chocolate: creamy chocolate sauce 33
  sauce, blender or processor recipe 47
cilantro lime sauce **24-25**, 28
cold Swedish sauce 16
cornstarch sauce 32
coulis 35
cream: general 36, 38
creamy chocolate sauce 33
Cumberland sauce 20
cumin tomato sauce 28
curry sauce 20
  blender or processor recipe 46
custard sauce 33, 38, **38**
  blender or processor recipe 47
Deglazing 7
dressings: French 40
  hot vinaigrette 23
  low-calorie 40
  sour cream 40
  vinaigrette 40, **41**
Eggs: egg whites 17
  Scotch egg sauce 28

Fines herbes 39
fish stock 8
flathead, fillets of (with cheese sauce) 26
French dressing 40
fudge sauce 35
Garlic sauce 22, **22**
Grand Marnier sauce 36
green tartare sauce 16
Gribiche sauce 18, **18**
Herb & cream sauce with noodles 26
hollandaise sauce 12, **13**
  blender or processor recipe 39
horseradish: cream 29
  fresh 40
  sauce 40
hot vinaigrette 23
Ice-cream cake with caramel sauce **34**, 35
Jam sauce 33
Lemon cucumber sauce 19
lemon sauce 47
  with melon 47
lime: cilantro lime sauce **24-25**, 28
light stock 8
low-calorie dressing 40
Mayonnaise 15
  blender or processor recipe 39
Melba sauce (berry coulis) 35
melon balls with lemon sauce **2**, 47
mint sauce 19
mornay sauce 11
mushroom sauce **14**, 15
Noodles, with Herb & cream sauce 26
Onion sauce 11
orange sauce 47
oyster sauce 11
Parsley sauce 11
pasta, with ricotta sauce 26, **27**
peach sauce 35
peanut sauce 22

pesto 44, **44-45**
piquant tomato sauce 30
Rarebit sauce 19
ravigot sauce 16
  blender or processor recipe 46
redfish, fillets of (with cheese sauce) 26
ricotta herb sauce 46
ricotta sauce with pasta 26, **27**
rum butter 38
Satay sauce 23
sauce-boats 18
sauce choron 13
sauce madère 10
sauce paloise 13
sauce poulette 15
sauce sabayon aux fruits 36, **37**
Scotch egg sauce 28
Sicilian tomato sauce 29
spices, ground: general 12
sour cream dressing 40
stocks, general 8
  brown 8, **9**
  fish 8
  light 8
Swedish sauce, cold 16
sweet & sour sauce **42**, 43
Tabasco sauce 29
tartare sauce 16,**17**
  green tartare sauce 16
tomatoes: general preparation 43
  tomato chartreuse with horseradish cream 29
  cumin & tomato sauce 28
  piquant tomato sauce 30
  tomato sauce 30, **30-31**
  Sicilian tomato sauce 29
Vanilla extract 12
velouté sauce (velvet sauce) 15
vinaigrette 40, **41**
  hot 23
White (béchamel) sauce 11
  basic white sauce 12
wine: burnt wine sauce 32
Zabaglione 36